CLASSROOM HOW-TO

GIVING A PRESENTATION

VALERIE BODDEN | ILLUSTRATIONS BY NATE WILLIAMS

CREATIVE 🍎 EDUCATION

Published by Creative Education
P.O. Box 227, Mankato, Minnesota 56002
Creative Education is an imprint of The Creative Company
www.thecreativecompany.us

Design and production by Liddy Walseth
Art direction by Rita Marshall
Printed in the United States of America

Illustrations by Nate Williams © 2014

Library of Congress Cataloging-in-Publication Data
Bodden, Valerie.
Giving a presentation / Valerie Bodden.
p. cm. — (Classroom how-to)
Includes bibliographical references and index.
Summary: An approachable guide to help master and apply the
writing, speaking, and listening skills involved in preparing for
and confidently delivering an effective presentation.
ISBN 978-1-60818-280-0
1. Public speaking—Juvenile literature. 2. Report writing—Juvenile
literature. I. Title.
PN4129.15.B64 2014
808.5'1—dc23   2013029619

CCSS: RI.5.1, 2, 3, 7, 8, 9; RH.6-8.1, 6, 9; W.5.1, 2, 3, 4, 5, 7, 8, 9, 10;
W.6.1, 2, 4, 7, 8, 9; SL.6.1, 3, 4, 6

First Edition
2 4 6 8 9 7 5 3 1

TABLE OF CONTENTS

HOMEWORK. *Tests.* Speeches. **Papers.**

Does it sometimes feel like you face an endless list of tasks to complete for school? And why? To make your teachers happy? Well, yes, completing your work is likely to make your teachers happy. But that is not the only reason teachers assign work. Believe it or not, writing papers, taking tests, and making speeches benefits you, too. Every time you complete one of these tasks, you learn something more about how to do it, and you become more prepared to do it again in the future—in high school, college, and even possibly your career. But more than that, these tasks teach you how to learn, how to study, how to find information, and how to present your viewpoint. And such skills will help you not only in the classroom but also in life.

Presentations, for example, can teach you how to get your point across clearly and with confidence when you are talking with others. And that's a skill that can be employed in nearly every aspect of your life—from giving a friend directions to your house to trying to convince your parents to let you stay out late. Of course, as with any new skill, learning to give a presentation takes information and practice. What should you talk about? Where do you get your research? What kinds of visual aids should you use? How do you deal with nerves? Learning the answers to these questions will help you deliver a presentation that will make your teacher happy—and teach you something in the process!

CHAPTER
ONE

DON'T SWEAT IT

Delivering a presentation combines the skills of writing and speaking. First you need to find and organize your information. Then you need to present it. Unlike a written paper, a presentation is intended to be heard rather than read. And that's what might scare you—the idea of getting up in front of a group and speaking. If so, take heart—public speaking is the number-one fear of many students and adults alike.

If most people are so afraid of public speaking, why does your teacher want you to do it? Well, for one, learning how to give a presentation now will make it less scary in the future. And you almost certainly *will* have to speak publicly in the future. Believe it or not, almost any career you might pursue will require some sort of speaking skills. Teachers, lawyers, doctors, business owners, politicians, scientists, and engineers all use public speaking skills at one time or another—some on a daily basis. And even if your future career doesn't demand that you speak to groups of people, you will likely need to talk to your boss from time to time—and it won't hurt to be able to **persuade** her to give you a raise!

But that's in the future. Right now, preparing a presentation will help you learn how to find, evaluate, and organize information. It will teach you to communicate clearly and to develop critical thinking skills. Critical thinking helps you determine whether an argument is sound, whether someone's opinion can be trusted, or whether one event really did cause another. This type of reasoning helps you to discover the relationships between ideas.

Presentations also serve a more immediate purpose. They allow you to interact with your audience. In some cases, you might inform your listeners about a subject that is new to them. Or you might teach them how to do something. In other cases, you will try to persuade listeners to change their mind or their actions or both. And your speech could even make a difference in their lives. Maybe you'll persuade a classmate to eat more healthfully, or maybe you'll inspire your whole class to start a recycling program or to hold a fundraiser for an important cause.

The good news is that you already have some of the skills needed for giving a presentation, even if you've never given one before in your life. How can that be? Many of the skills needed for presentations are ones that are also used in everyday conversations. When you talk with someone, you think about who that person is before choosing the topic of conversation and even the words you use. For example, if you are talking to your teacher, you probably won't mention how you blew off your homework to play a video game. But with a group of friends, you might celebrate the fact that you made it to level 15, peppering your conversation with all sorts of slang words that you wouldn't use when talking with your teacher or another adult because—let's face

"YOU CAN HAVE BRILLIANT IDEAS, BUT IF YOU CAN'T GET THEM ACROSS, YOUR BRAINS WON'T GET YOU ANYWHERE."

— Lee Iacocca

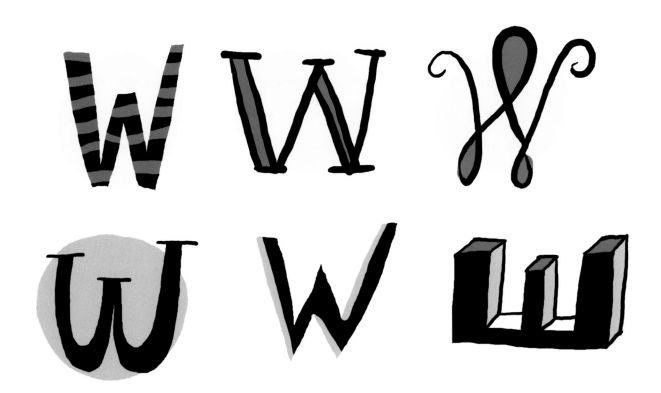

WORK DOESN'T STOP THERE

it—they just wouldn't get it. Considering your listeners, or audience, when choosing a topic is important in public speaking as well—so there's one skill you can check off your list.

As you speak in everyday conversation, you also organize your thoughts—probably without even realizing it. If you want to teach someone how to do something, for example, you tell her the steps in order, not randomly. And if you want to convince her that your point of view is correct, you present a logical argument. In public speaking, organized thinking enables the audience to follow your reasoning and understand your point.

Another public speaking skill we all use every day is storytelling. We tell about something funny that happened in the cafeteria, a dramatic play at a basketball game, or a great movie we watched over the weekend. And we tell those stories in a way that gets the listener involved: by raising or lowering our voice, using gestures, and building to the climax. Skillful speakers do the same in presentations, relating their information in a way that grabs and holds the audience's attention. So you see, you're already on your way to becoming a successful public speaker, just on the basis of the skills you use in everyday conversation!

However, some aspects of public speaking do present challenges to most people. One of the biggest is nerves. Even if you're comfortable telling a story to a large group of friends gathered around your locker, you may become frightened at the thought of getting up in front of those same people in the classroom. But feeling nervous is not necessarily a bad thing—it just means that your **adrenaline** is pumping as you get ready for the big moment. And, dealt with in the right way, nerves can even help you deliver a dynamic, energetic speech.

Another challenge to some students is the preparation that goes say. As you give your first presentations, you will face the challenges of speaking loudly and clearly, making eye contact with your audience, conveying enthusiasm for your subject, and avoiding distractions such as playing with your hair or repeating meaningless words such as "um." Don't worry, though—the more presentations you give, the easier these habits will become. So push past your fears and get ready to start talking!

CHALLENGE

into making a speech. While in conversation, you may spend a few seconds composing your answer to another's comment. But for a presentation, you will likely spend days—if not weeks— preparing, sorting through information and organizing it in a way that will make sense to listeners.

And the work doesn't stop there. After you've prepared your speech, you need to *deliver* your information. In many cases, *how* you deliver your content may have nearly as much impact on your listeners as *what* you

CHAPTER
TWO

SOMETHING TO TALK ABOUT

Of course, before you can talk, you need something to talk about. In other words, you need a topic. In some cases, your teacher may assign one. If he tells you to give a speech about starfish, for example, then that's what you'll give a speech about. In other cases, your teacher may simply direct you to give a presentation related to a general subject area, leaving the choice of the specific topic to you. If your teacher wants a speech about the ocean, you'll need to decide which aspects of the ocean to cover—sea life, underwater volcanoes, or water pollution, for example.

Sometimes, your teacher may even leave the choice of topic entire-ly up to you. Sounds perfect, right? For some people, yes. For others, the opportunity to choose a topic presents a huge challenge. After all, the world is full of subjects—how can you possibly narrow down the choices? If you find yourself in this situation, don't fret. Answering the following questions will help you find a perfect topic in no time:

1. What are your interests?

2. Who is your audience?

3. What kind of speech do you need to give?

In order to give an interesting speech, you need to be interested in your topic. This may seem obvious, but what if you can't think of some-

"THE PROBLEM OF EDUCATION IS TWO-FOLD; FIRST TO KNOW, AND THEN TO UTTER."

— Robert Louis Stevenson

thing worthy of a speech? If nothing pops immediately into your head, try brainstorming. Make a list of all the things you enjoy doing, the places you like to go, the people you find fascinating. You can also list things you know a lot about or things you'd like to learn more about. If that doesn't work, take a stroll through the library, page through an encyclopedia, or browse the Internet.

Once you have a list of ideas, look through it with a critical eye. Do any seem like potential speech topics? Perhaps you've identified a general subject area, such as Afghanistan. That's a big subject, though—one that would take you many days to discuss in full. Since your teacher has probably set a shorter time limit on

your speech (maybe 5 to 10 minutes), you need to narrow your topic. Perhaps you are interested in the country's customs, or maybe you want to talk about American military involvement there. Maybe what really fascinates you is the region's geography.

In addition to considering your own interests as you choose a topic, you should think about what is likely to interest your audience. Consider your listeners' age, gender, education, and profession. Of course, for school, you will most likely be speaking to your teacher and your classmates. With the exception of your teacher, your audience will be people your own age. Does it matter if your class is made up mostly of boys or girls? Maybe. It depends on each person's specific interests (many of which you probably already know from being around your classmates every day).

But what if you need to give a speech outside the classroom? Maybe you have been asked to talk to the school board, for example. Now you are addressing an older audience. Most of your listeners will probably be well-educated, professional people. Since they are members of the school board, you know they have an interest in education. With those character-

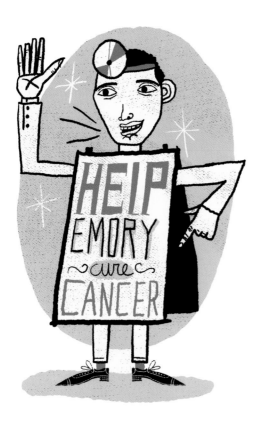

istics in mind, you might choose to speak about your school's need for a new computer lab, or you might propose an award system for students who make the honor roll. You probably wouldn't speak about the awesome new skate park down the road.

Finally, the type of speech your teacher has assigned will help guide your choice of topic. In most cases, you will be asked to give either an informative or a persuasive speech. As its name suggests, an informative speech is intended to inform, or tell, the audience about something. You might use an informative speech to demonstrate how to do something, such as making a snowman. An in-

formative speech can also teach the audience about an event (such as the sinking of the *Titanic*), an object (such as a submarine), or even a hobby (such as canoeing).

A persuasive speech, on the other hand, is intended to convince the audience that your point of view is correct. In many cases, it also seeks to get the audience to take a specific action. Persuasive speeches usually deal with controversial topics—ones that have at least two opposing viewpoints. Gun control, the death penalty, and abortion are controversial issues in society at large. But persuasive speeches don't have to deal with national controversies. You can probably find controversial issues right in your own city (whether to build a new library), school (whether to cut funding from the art program), or even home (whether to get a dog).

Once you've chosen your topic, it's time to gather the information you'll need to speak about it. In some cases, this information may come from your own head. If you're an accomplished skier and your speech is about how to ski, for example, you will rely on your own experience as you speak. Using such personal examples can help to draw listeners into your speech.

TEACHER, LIBRARIAN

In many cases, however, your teacher will require that your presentation include research. Backing your speech up with information drawn from other sources helps to give you **credibility**. Conducting research for a presentation is basically the same as conducting research for a paper. As you begin your search, it can help to get an overview of your topic in a general reference work such as an encyclopedia. Once you are familiar with the topic and its terminology, you can turn to books, magazines, and **journal** articles for more detailed information. You'll probably have to make a trip to the library to pick up books, but many libraries allow you to access articles from periodicals (magazines, newspapers, and journals), as well as some encyclopedias, through online

databases. If you are unfamiliar with how to do so, your librarian will be happy to teach you. Depending on your topic, you might also want to conduct an interview as part of your research process. If you are researching the long-term effects of combat on soldiers, for example, interviewing a veteran can lend a personal touch to your information.

The Internet can also be a good source of information for many topics, especially those dealing with current issues that may not yet have been covered by print resources. As you use the Internet, though, keep in mind that not all the information it contains is equally accurate. Before using information from a specific Web page, evaluate whether it is reliable. Does the site list an author? Can you check his **credentials**? When was the page last updated? Who sponsors the

page (a government agency or educational institution, or a company trying to get your business)?

As you gather information, you will need a way to keep track of it. And, no, your memory is not sufficient. (Try to remember what you wore to school last Tuesday and you'll see why.) Researchers use a number of different note-taking systems, and unless your teacher specifies which to use, you can choose the one that works best for you. Some people prefer to take notes on index cards. The idea is to write one note per card. That way, when you are done taking notes, you can easily shuffle the cards into a logical order. Or you could write your notes in a research notebook, dedicating a separate page to information from each source. Another version of the research notebook uses a separate page for notes on each main point. If you don't like writing notes longhand, you can keep your notes in a computer file. Like the research notebook, this method allows you to use a separate page for each source or for each main point.

Whichever method of note-taking you choose, be sure to keep track of each note's source. This will not only make it easier for you to double-check information later, but it will also make referring to your sources during the course of your presentation a snap. In addition, if you note an author's exact words, be sure to put them in quotation marks so that you don't later **plagiarize** and use the words as if they were your own.

KEEP YOUR NOTES IN A COMPUTER FILE

Your teacher will probably also want to see a **bibliography** of the sources you used in preparing your presentation. So be sure to note the author's name, title, city of publication, publisher, and date of publication for every book you use. For articles, note the author's name, the article title, the periodical title, the date published, and the page numbers on which the article appears. Your teacher will likely specify a format in which to present this information, or you can refer to a handbook such as the *MLA Handbook for Writers of Research Papers* for instructions. If writing a bibliography at first seems complicated, don't panic—like every step of the presentation process, it will get easier with practice.

CHAPTER
THREE

MAKING A PLAN

At this point in your speaking career, your teacher will likely require that you write out your entire presentation before delivering it. As you become a more experienced speaker, you may find that you are able to develop your presentation based on an outline, without actually writing down everything you will say.

As you prepare your presentation, keep in mind that organization is key. A reader perusing a report can always reread something that doesn't make sense to her, but someone listening to your speech does not have that luxury. One way to organize your information before writing is to create an outline.

Traditionally, an outline employs roman numerals (such as I, V, and X), letters, and arabic numerals, as in the following:

I. Tornado Safety
   A. Before
      1. Listen for weather warnings
      2. Watch the sky
   B. During
      1. Take shelter in a basement or interior room
      2. If outdoors, get indoors, into a vehicle, or to a low-lying spot
   C. After
      1. Get out of damaged buildings
      2. Watch out for downed power lines

The roman numerals in an outline

a **rhetorical** question such as "If you found $100 on the sidewalk, what would you do with it?"

Once you've captured your audience's attention, you need to let them know exactly what you will be speaking about. For example, is your rhetorical question about finding $100 leading to a speech about honesty, about spending versus saving money, or about what you can buy for $100 these days? Your introduction should also let listeners know why this topic is important. Often, the introduction ends with a brief statement that previews what you will cover in the body of the speech.

The body is where you make your main points. Most presentations have

represent main points, or topic sentences. The capital letters list sub-points under each main point, and the arabic numerals detail additional information and supporting materials under each sub-point. Although this is the standard format for an outline, yours can be less formal. Right now, the main goal is simply to impose some order on your ideas.

Once you've done that, you can begin to write. As you do so, keep in mind that every speech has three main parts: the introduction, the body, and the conclusion. The first job of the introduction is to grab your listeners' attention. If you fail to do that here, you are not likely to get it later. So think carefully about your opening lines. You might start with a compelling story, a startling fact, or an interesting quotation. Or you could ask your audience

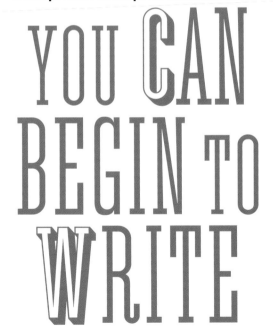

YOU CAN BEGIN TO WRITE

two to five main points. You probably won't have time to cover more, and even if you do, listeners might have a hard time remembering more than that. Your main points need to be presented in a logical order—and this order can vary, depending on your topic. The most logical organization for topics dealing with events or processes (such as a "how-to" speech) is probably chronological, or in the order in which you do each step. Spatial organization might work best for other speeches, such as one in which you discuss the elements of a work of art from left to right, for example. Some speeches describe a cause followed by its effect (or vice versa) or a problem followed by a solution. For persuasive speeches, you might start with your weakest argument and end with your strongest.

The body of your speech is also where you support your main points with examples and other information. This does not mean simply rattling off a list of everything you discovered throughout the course of your research. Instead, you need to consider

which information will best support each of your points. Among the most effective types of support are examples, statistics, and quotations.

Examples can help clarify an idea and bring it to life. That's why this book is filled with examples of presentation topics and situations. Often, examples are brief—only a sentence or two long. Other examples are longer. They might relate an entire story (which is why they are sometimes referred to as **anecdotes** or illustrations). These examples are rich in detail and can help to add a human touch to your presentation. They might tug at listeners' emotions, making them feel sad, angry, hopeful, or anxious. Examples don't necessarily have to be real, either. You can use **hypothetical** examples as well; just don't try to trick your audience into thinking such examples are real.

Often, examples can be made even more effective by following them with statistics. Statistics can help to prove that your example is one instance of a wider issue. Maybe you give an example about Amanda, a young adult who can't read. After your example, you might say, "Sadly, Amanda is not alone. According to the United States Department of Education, in 2009,

one in seven American adults could not read above a basic level." Whether used with an example or alone, you need to be careful when presenting statistics. Remember that your listeners cannot rewind to hear you rattle off a list of numbers again. Throwing figure after figure at your audience is likely to cause eyes to glaze over. So choose your statistics carefully. And be sure to interpret them for your listeners. For example, the statement that cardiovascular disease kills about 600,000 Americans each year might not mean much to listeners. But if you put that number in context, it might have a greater impact: "That means that 68 people in this country die of cardiovascular disease every hour."

Another powerful source of support is testimony. When you use testimony, you quote or paraphrase what some-

one else has to say about your topic. In many cases, you will give expert testimony. This can help to prove that your ideas are backed up by experts in the field. Sometimes, you might also choose to include peer testimony, or the opinions of people like yourself (or like your audience) who have firsthand experience with your topic. Although peer testimony doesn't prove your point, it does give a personal touch to your information. Whether you use

main points, you shouldn't simply stop talking. Instead, you need to bring your speech to a satisfying conclusion. Your conclusion may summarize your main points or remind listeners of why your topic is important. Keep in mind that your conclusion is the last impression you will leave on your audience, so take time to come up with a memorable ending. You might incorporate a powerful quote, direct the audience to think of what your topic means for the future, or call for audience

SHOW YOUR AUDIENCE

expert or peer testimony, be sure to acknowledge your source. In fact, the same is true for any type of support you use from outside sources. That acknowledgement can be as simple as an introductory statement, such as "Abraham Lincoln once said, ..." or "According to local librarian Brenda Davis, ..."

When you have made all your

members to take action (especially for persuasive speeches). Sometimes, the most effective conclusions refer back to the introduction, bringing the speech full circle.

As you write your entire presentation, keep in mind that you will eventually deliver it. So write it the way you speak. Don't try to sound "smart"

"EDUCATION IS ABOUT ... LEARNING TO SAVOR THE QUALITY OF THE JOURNEY. IT IS ABOUT INQUIRY AND DELIBERATION. IT IS ABOUT BECOMING CRITICALLY MINDED AND INTELLECTU- ALLY CURIOUS, AND IT IS ABOUT LEARNING HOW TO FRAME AND PURSUE YOUR OWN EDUCATIONAL AIMS."

— Elliot W. Eisner

by using big words or complicated sentence structures. These will only serve to confuse listeners. Instead, pay close attention to the rhythm of your words. If you can't "hear" the rhythm in your head, try reading your speech out loud. Fix areas that sound awkward (or that create unintentional tongue twisters). As you edit, or make changes, be sure to also time yourself reading your speech out loud. Make sure that it fits within the time limits your teacher has set—if it doesn't, cut or add information as needed.

think about places where you might incorporate visual aids. Props, or physical objects, can often benefit an informative speech. If you are talking about how to put on football gear, for example, it will help tremendously if you actually have that gear with you and can show as you tell. Other types of visual aids include posters and computer-generated slide shows. These types of visual aids might provide lists to help listeners follow a sequence of events or charts and graphs to make statistical information easier to under-

Although presentations are meant to be heard rather than read, they do sometimes have visual elements, known as visual aids. A visual aid is anything you show your audience in order to help make your point clearer. Visual aids can also benefit your speech by grabbing your listeners' attention and helping them to remember your points. So, as you write your speech,

stand. In some cases, you might even use video clips as visual aids. Whatever type of visual aids you use, be sure that they are large enough and clear enough for everyone to see and read.

Once you've finished organizing your information, drafting your speech, and preparing your visual aids, there's really only one thing left to do: deliver your presentation!

STAND UP AND SPEAK

So far, you've spent a lot of time researching and writing, so you may think that you're ready to give your presentation. Almost. But first, you need to practice. Why? Few people are comfortable talking in front of a group without first rehearsing what they are going to say—and *how* they are going to say it. In fact, how you give your presentation is often just as important as what you say. You may have written a superb speech, but if you deliver it poorly, it will fall flat. You might distract, confuse, or even lose listeners' attention altogether.

Before you begin to practice, you should decide whether you are going to read directly from your paper, memorize your speech, or use notes. Chances are, your teacher does not want you to simply read your written report out loud (otherwise she would have assigned a paper rather than a presentation). Although some teachers may expect students to memorize short speeches, most likely your teacher will allow you to use notes to jog your memory. So, you need to prepare those notes. Index cards can work well, as long as you don't drop them (in which case picking them up and putting them back in order would be a distraction to both you and your listeners). To avoid this risk, you might instead use a speaking outline—a basic outline of your main points, written on a single sheet of paper that you can set on a podium or lectern.

Whichever method you use, the idea is not to cram your entire speech into your notes but rather to include important phrases and key words to

CONVERSATIONAL RATHER THAN STIFF

remind yourself of the ideas you want to cover. You might also write down statistics or full quotations to ensure that you deliver them accurately. Your notes can also include delivery directions. For example, if you want to make sure to emphasize a certain point, you might highlight it. Or you might make yourself a note to speak more slowly at a dramatic point in your presentation. In addition, you will probably want to make note of where to use each of your visual aids so that you don't accidentally skip one during your presentation.

As you practice using your notes, you don't need to try to remember the exact words you used in the written copy of your presentation. In fact, you will probably find that each time you give your speech, your wording is a little bit different. That's okay. Deciding on your exact words as you speak will help your presentation feel fresh and conversational rather than stiff and scripted.

Once you have practiced your presentation several times on your own, you might ask your family or friends to listen to it and give you feedback. They can let you know if any parts of it confuse them, if you are distracting listeners with your mannerisms (swaying back and forth, for example), or if you are speaking slowly enough. Some people like to practice in front of a mirror or to videotape themselves and then critique their performance as well. You might also find it helpful to practice delivering your speech in your empty classroom before you have to perform the real thing.

By the time you have practiced your speech a number of times, you will probably feel fairly comfortable with the information you have to present on the big day. And that should help to calm your nerves. But you still may not feel completely at ease as you get up in front of your classmates and teacher. And that's fine. Before you walk to the front of the room, remind yourself that you have written a good speech and practiced it thoroughly and that you are ready for this. When you get to the front of the room, take a moment to confidently look out at your audience. Don't apologize for being nervous. Your listeners probably can't tell that you're nervous, so there's no reason to let them know that you are. Plus, if you act like you're not nervous, you'll start to feel less nervous. So, take a

deep breath and begin to speak. As you get going, you'll get so caught up in the excitement of delivering your information that your nerves will fade into the background.

As you deliver your presentation, pay close attention to how you use your voice. You want to make sure that your audience can understand you. So speak slowly and **enunciate** carefully. Make sure everyone can hear you (without shouting), and don't be afraid to vary your volume, rate, and **pitch** throughout the speech in order to avoid putting your audience to sleep with a **monotone**. At times, it is appropriate to speak more loudly or softly to emphasize your point. Or you might increase your speaking rate as you approach an exciting moment. You can even insert pauses for dramatic effect. Varying the pitch of your voice can convey your feelings toward the subject.

Although your voice is your primary tool for delivering your presentation, what you do with the rest of your body matters as well. Your eyes, for

"ONE WHO FORMS A JUDGMENT ON ANY POINT BUT CANNOT EXPLAIN IT MIGHT AS WELL NEVER HAVE THOUGHT AT ALL ON THE SUBJECT."

— *Pericles*

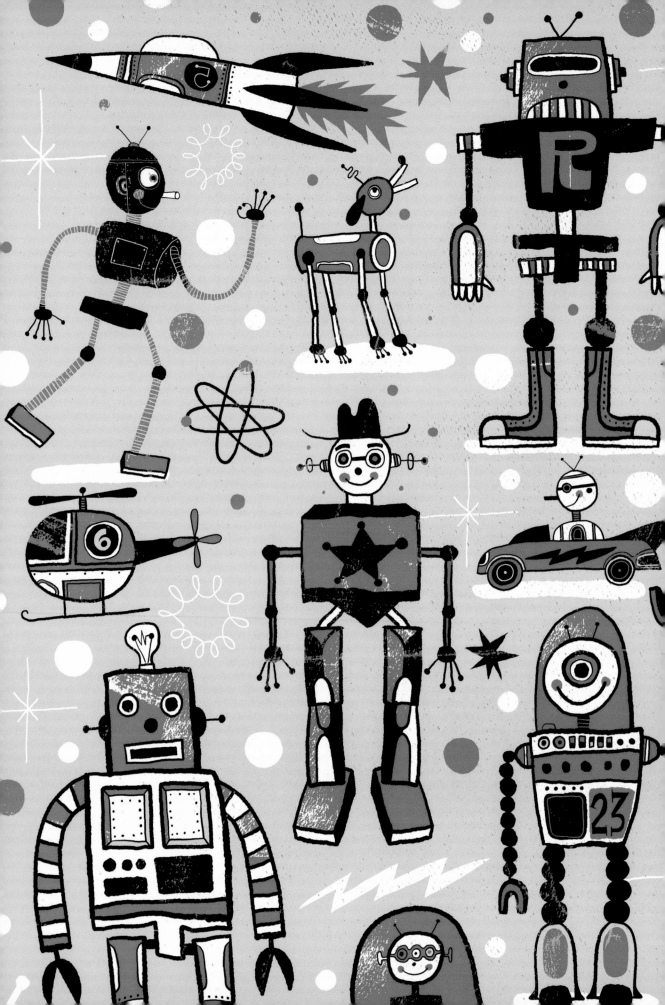

example, should not be glued to your notes. Instead, look out at your listeners and make eye contact with them. This helps to establish a connection between yourself and the individuals in the audience. It also makes you seem more credible and trustworthy. (How do you feel about someone who won't look you in the eye when he talks to you?) At the same time, make sure that your facial expression matches what you are saying. If you are talking about a subject that gives you joy (basketball, perhaps), smile and show enthusiasm. If, on the other hand, you are talking about a serious topic such as poverty, make sure that your face reflects concern or thoughtfulness.

Many beginning speakers wonder what to do with their hands as they talk. First, let's talk about what not to do: don't play with your notes, clasp and unclasp your fingers, or twirl your rings. Instead, let your arms hang comfortably at your sides. And, when it feels natural, use them to gesture.

How? Well, think about how you use your hands in everyday conversation, and you'll realize that you already know how to gesture. You can use your hands to indicate size, to emphasize an idea (think clenched fist), or to enumerate points (holding up two fingers when talking about the second item in a list, for example).

As for what to do with the rest of your body, stand up straight, for starters. Even if you don't mean to give the impression, slouching indicates that you aren't particularly enthused about your presentation. If you're standing behind a podium or lectern, you may choose to stay in one spot throughout your speech. Or you can come out from behind the podium and move around a bit. This doesn't mean you should pace back and forth across the front of the room—that would distract listeners. But you can take a few steps to one side or the other as you **transition** from one idea to the next.

So your voice and body movements are under control. Now, what

about incorporating visual aids? Whenever you show a new visual aid, be sure to give your audience time to look at it. Even as your listeners are looking at your aid, however, you should still be looking at—and talking to—your listeners. Don't make the mistake of turning your back on them to talk to your visual aid. If there are words on your visual aid, don't simply read them **verbatim**. Instead, briefly explain the visual if necessary. When you are done with a specific visual aid, put it away (if it's a physical object), cover it up (if it's a poster), or turn it off (if it's a computer slide). Otherwise, listeners may continue to focus on your visual aid rather than on you.

Even if you pay the most careful attention to practicing your speech, controlling your voice and body movements, and using your visual aids properly, something may still go wrong during the course of your presentation. Maybe you'll accidentally mispronounce a word or skip a point. Or maybe the projector you need to show your visual aid won't work. Don't panic. Instead, just keep going. If you can correct yourself without interrupting the flow of your speech (re-pronouncing a word, for example), do so. Otherwise, ignore the mistake. Chances are, your listeners won't even notice. And if they do, they'll respect you for taking it in stride and handling it like a professional.

After you've finished your speech,

A NEW SET OF SKILLS

take a moment to look out at your audience, thank them, and then slowly return to your seat. And then relax: you've done it! You've collected research, organized information, and delivered a dynamic presentation that would make any teacher smile. And it should make you smile, too; after all, you've learned a new set of skills that you'll be able to make use of for the rest of your life!

GLOSSARY

adrenaline: a hormone released into the body in response to stress or fear, causing an increase in heart rate and blood pressure

anecdotes: brief stories recounting a specific incident or event

bibliography: a list of sources (such as books, articles, and websites) consulted in the course of writing a research paper, article, or book

credentials: a list of qualifications (such as degrees earned or awards received) that reflects a person's area of expertise

credibility: the quality of being believable

databases: organized collections of data, or information, stored on a computer

enunciate: to pronounce clearly

hypothetical: made up or based on assumptions and possibilities rather than actual facts or situations

journal: a publication, often scholarly in nature, that typically contains articles related to a specific field of study

monotone: a voice that does not vary in pitch or tone

persuade: to try to convince someone to believe or do something

pitch: the highness or lowness of a person's voice

plagiarize: to take credit for another person's thoughts or words

rhetorical: asked for the purpose of making a point rather than to be answered

transition: to move from one idea to another

verbatim: word for word

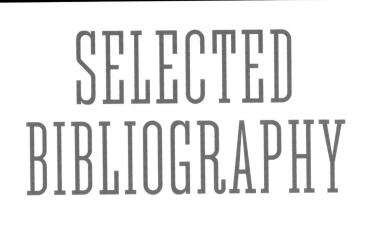

SELECTED BIBLIOGRAPHY

Arnold, Kristin. *Boring to Bravo: Proven Presentation Techniques to Engage, Involve, and Inspire Your Audience to Action.* Austin, Tex.: Greenleaf Book Group Press, 2010.

Book Builders LLC. *How to Write a Great Research Paper.* Hoboken, N.J.: J. Wiley & Sons, 2004.

Frank, Steven. *Public Speaking: Proven Techniques for Giving Successful Talks Every Time.* Holbrook, Mass.: Adams Media Corporation, 2000.

Kline, John A. *Speaking Effectively: Achieving Excellence in Presentations.* Upper Saddle River, N.J.: Pearson/Prentice Hall, 2004.

Lucas, Stephen E. *The Art of Public Speaking.* 11th ed. Boston: McGraw-Hill, 2012.

Turabian, Kate L. *A Manual for Writers of Research Papers, Theses, and Dissertations: Chicago Style for Students and Researchers.* 7th ed. Chicago: University of Chicago Press, 2007.

Wong, Dona M. The Wall Street Journal *Guide to Information Graphics: The Dos and Don'ts of Presenting Data, Facts, and Figures.* New York: W. W. Norton, 2010.

READ MORE

Bodden, Valerie. *Effective Speeches.* Mankato, Minn.: Creative Education, 2011.

Dyett-Welcome, Michelle J. *Excuse Me! Let Me Speak! A Young Person's Guide to Public Speaking.* Bloomington, Ind.: AuthorHouse, 2009.

Gallagher, Michael. *Speaking Out: An Introduction to Public Speaking; A Student-Friendly Guide to Public Speaking.* Colorado Springs: Meriwether, 2010.

McIntire, Suzanne, ed. *American Heritage Book of Great American Speeches for Young People.* New York: Wiley, 2001.

WEBSITES

American Rhetoric
http://www.americanrhetoric.com/
Get inspired for your own presentation by reading or listening to some of the world's most famous speeches.

Toastmasters International Tips & Techniques
http://www.toastmasters.org/MainMenuCategories/
FreeResources/NeedHelpGivingaSpeech/TipsTechniques.aspx
Find tips for using visual aids, gesturing, and incorporating humor into your presentations.

Your Voice! Public Speaking for Teens
http://www.facebook.com/pages/Your-Voice-Public-Speaking-for-Teens/150070651720209
Watch videos of teenage speakers and critique their performances.

Note: Every effort has been made to ensure that the websites listed above are suitable for children, that they have educational value, and that they contain no inappropriate material. However, because of the nature of the Internet, it is impossible to guarantee that these sites will remain active indefinitely or that their contents will not be altered.

INDEX